An Educational Blueprint

Teachers-Parents Partnering
for Student Success

An Educational Blueprint

Teachers-Parents Partnering for Student Success

Debra Tavaras, Bevin Carpenter, et al.

Soulstice, Inc.

Atlanta

"Thank you for supporting this book!" A portion of the proceeds will go towards sustaining programs with Soulstice Inc., helping us encourage change by empowering the next generation of leaders. Your purchase makes a difference!

For Information about workshops or speaking engagements please contact: soulsticeinc10@gmail.com.

www.soulsticeinc.org

Credits:

Book Interior Design: Laura Lis Scott, BookLove.Space

Cover Design and Graphic Artist: Justin Douglas, jrdgds@gmail.com

Special Thanks:

The Annie Casey Foundation for their continued support.

ISBN: 979-8-218-48445-3

CONTENTS

PREFACE

An Educational Blueprint: Teachers-Parents Partnering for Student Success is a book that outlines the cornerstone of education. Parents and educators are the two biggest support structures that a child has, and they must work together in order for them to reach the pinnacle of their educational journey.

Why Educational Blueprint? The word "education" comes from multiple Latin words, including educare, educere, educo, and educatum. Educare has several meanings "to bring up" "to nourish" "to train," "to mold," as well as to encourage the growth and development of. Edecatum means "act of teaching or instruction." Blueprint: means "a plan that describes how to do or achieve something in the future"

The basis of the book comes from the question: What happens when we truly understand and leverage the insights and perspectives of teachers and parents in a child's educational journey? By exploring a series of questions with teachers, parents, and students, this book aims to provide a guide for fostering effective partnerships that will propel students towards academic success.

Our hope is to create a blueprint that highlights successful practices as well as strengthen the commitment to teamwork and communication. The goal is to empower educators, parents, and students with tools and insights that cultivate an approach which promotes student achievement.

We invite you to reflect on your own role in the educational ecosystem and to actively engage with the ideas found in this book. Teachers, parents, and students together can build a future where collaboration will be a tangible and transformative force in education.

Welcome to *An Educational Blueprint: Teachers-Parents Partnering for Student Success.* Your journey toward a more effective and empathetic partnership in education begins here!

Bevin Carpenter
CEO Building Bridges Consulting LLC

An Educational Blueprint

Introduction

Education serves as the foundation for personal and societal progress, shaping future leaders and innovators. In a world that demands constant adaptation and learning, it is important that teachers and parents collaborate by creating an environment where students can excel academically. *"An Educational Blueprint: Teachers-Parents Partnering for Student Success"* provides a guide for creating an environment that emphasizes the power of collaboration.

Teachers and parents face a number of challenges that have hindered student success. Technology has transformed how students learn and interact; this means that it is necessary for educators and parents to continuously adapt. Teachers must integrate technology into their curriculum while making sure that it is being used effectively and responsibly. Parents should guide their children on engaging with technology in more constructive and enriching ways.

Another challenge is the emphasis on standardized tests and academic performance, resulting in a curriculum that is focused on test preparation rather than a holistic approach to education. Teachers need to meet standards while developing students' skills in creativity, critical thinking, and emotional intelligence. Parents are concerned about their child's academic performance and what opportunities they will have in the future. This stress can lead to unrealistic expectations, which adds pressure on students. Communication between educators and parents is essential to help solidify a balanced approach to their children's education.

Diversity in the classroom presents another challenge. Schools are more culturally and linguistically diverse than ever before. While this opens opportunities to increase students' learning experiences, it also presents challenges in meeting everyone's educational needs. Teachers must develop culturally responsive teaching practices, and parents bear the responsibility for supporting their children's understanding and acceptance of diversity. Collaboration can create an inclusive environment where every student feels valued and supported as well as strengthening their social and academic success.

The pandemic disrupted education systems worldwide. Schools closed, thrusting educators and parents into uncharted territory: remote learning. With limited training, teachers had to adapt fast to online teaching. They had to master the technology and find ways to engage students, all while dealing with the impact the pandemic was having in their own homes. It was hard for educators to assess students' progress and maintain classroom management virtually. Parents became co-educators, taking on responsibilities for their children's learning while managing their own work -home situation.

The pandemic highlighted the importance of collaboration between educators and parents, who had to find ways to communicate to support students' academic and emotional well-being. Parents gained an insight into what teachers go through on a daily basis, and teachers came to appreciate just how important it is for parents to be actively involved in their children's education.

Hybrid teaching models and the consistent integration of technology in the classroom will likely continue. The pandemic has reinforced that fact that student success is best achieved when educators and parents work together to create a supportive and resilient educational environment.

Teachers guide students through their academic journey. Their expertise, dedication, and innovative teaching strategies are important to help students learn complex concepts and improve critical thinking skills. Parents are the first educators in a child's life. As primary caregivers and role models, they have an impact on their children's academic success. Their support and involvement will reinforce what happens in the classroom.

This guide shares effective collaboration strategies that teachers can use to enhance student engagement, and strategies for parents to be more involved with their children's educational journey, creating a conducive learning environment at home and maintaining communication with educators. By working together, educators and parents can create an ideal support system for students' academic and personal growth.

Collaboration between educators and parents provides a consistent and unified approach to education. Working together can reinforce positive behaviors, set realistic goals, and provide encouragement to guide students through their academic journey. While collaboration between educators and parents is important, students themselves must take accountability for their learning, *"An Educational Blueprint: Teachers–Parents Partnering for Student Success"* includes tips specifically for students, encouraging them to set realistic academic goals, develop effective study habits, and be responsible for their educational pursuits. By encouraging a sense of ownership and accountability, educators and parents can instill the skills students need to not only succeed in school but also in life.

PASSION AND PURPOSE

Choosing Education

The decision to pursue a career in education exceeds just being a profession, it is a commitment to shaping future generations. Educators serve as the architects of knowledge, molding young minds into empowered individuals capable of succeeding in a complex world. Their influence extends outside the classroom; they encourage members of society to value learning and strive to be productive citizens.

Education as a career is a powerful way for individuals to contribute to societal progress. Teachers are advocates for social change, breaking down barriers by providing equal access to education regardless of a student's socio-economic background. Educators equip students with skills needed to succeed and actively participate in a globalized economy.

Individuals choose a career in education for a number of reasons, quite a few are personal and driven by a passion to make a difference.

Here are a few key reasons:

> ➤ Many have a love for learning and a desire to share that love with others. They find happiness in teaching others.

> They desire a chance to influence and shape the future of others. Individuals thrive on helping others grow academically, socially, and emotionally.

> They carry a strong sense of social responsibility.

> They were inspired by their own teachers and/or mentors.

> They are drawn to teaching as a stable career with benefits. Stability attracts individuals looking for a reliable career path.

> They are interested in working as educators to inspire individuals with innovative ideas and innovative methodologies. This keeps the profession exciting.

> They like the variety of career paths in education. One can become a classroom teacher, counselor, work with special education, or become an administrator. With a variety to choose from, one can cultivate their interests.

The journey to become an educator is as unique as the individual. Each person brings a vast amount of experience, creative ways to motivate, and dreams of making a positive impact.

Below, three remarkable educators discuss why they chose education and why they stay. Despite their different paths, they share a dedication to making a difference through education.

First, we meet **Andrea**, She writes:

> I knew at an early age that I wanted to become a teacher. I would always want to play school, and I would get up early just to watch this show called *Romper Room.* I was excited about having the opportunity to enhance students' knowledge, as well as learning from the youth. I look forward to interactions, conversations, and creating new experiences every day.

Next, there is **Reggie**, who shares:

> I chose education because I wanted to have a positive impact on youth, setting positive examples for males, especially males of color.
>
> Every day in the field of education is a new day and a fresh start. You never know the influence you have in someone's life until you run into them later, and they tell you what is going on in their lives and remind you about something you said to them and how it made a positive impact on their lives. Whether you see them walk across the stage or their parents come up to you and thank you, moments like these consistently remind me why I am in this field.

Finally, we introduce **Kristy**. She says that:

> The person who inspired me and pointed me in the direction of education was my great aunt. She took me in, cared for and nurtured me. She loved me like I was her own child. I

would call her momma and my biological mother by her first name. My great aunt, momma, was the best thing that could have happened to me. She always saw the best in me, and if I had a problem or doubts about myself, she would always say, "There is no one smarter than you. Keep trying because I love you and that beautiful brain." Both of my parents were grateful that she was there for me."

These three educators, each with their unique journey, show the diverse paths that led them in education. Their stories illustrate how the field of education is enriched by the wide range of experiences and backgrounds of individuals who dedicate themselves to making a difference.

Choosing education as a career is not just about imparting knowledge, but about having a positive impact with future generations. This requires a commitment to developing students' talents, encouraging growth, and preparing students to succeed in school and in life.

ENVISIONING THE FUTURE

One Transformational Change in Education

Education is always evolving; however, educators agree that there is always room for improvement. Given one chance to make a change, those who are passionate about education think about solutions to challenges that will enhance the learning experience for students.

We asked our educators what changes would they would like to see:

Reggie:

I would love to see parents more involved, and students being held accountable. My thought is by not holding students accountable, we are setting them up for failure. Parents not becoming more involved is one reason our education system is in the shape that it is. We have to stop making excuses and take a more active role. Society does not care about anything other than that you are a positive, productive citizen.

Andrea:

I would like to see the education system stay consistent. There are always changes, and this can be overwhelming. It makes it hard to plan, therefore it does have a direct impact on students' learning.

One issue that keeps coming up since the pandemic is the need for comprehensive mental health support within the education system. Mental health is so important in students' well-being and academic success; however, it is still not addressed in schools. Schools that provide access to counselors, mental health education for both students and parents, and resources that addresses stress management can create a more supportive environment that takes a holistic approach. Addressing mental health issues strengthens students' academic achievement and provides them with the tools to manage their emotional challenges that will help them in school, home, and their community.

Another change that could transform education is shifting to personalized learning and getting away from the one-size-fits-all teaching methods. The one-size-fits-all approach fails to meet the students' diverse needs and learning styles. Encouraging educators to incorporate more innovative teaching strategies will enable them to tailor instruction to each student's strengths, interests, and pace of learning. By taking this approach, not only it will address the needs of the learner, but it also gets them ready for the changing world, where adaptability and continual learning is so important.

Given one chance to implement a change in education, thoughts should be to create a more inclusive, supportive, and personalized learning environment.

The future of education will depend on educators being able to adapt and innovate, making sure that future generations will succeed academically.

DESIGNING THE IDEAL SCHOOL

Fostering Strong Teacher-Student Relationship

Educators have great ideas of what an ideal school would look like. One can envision a learning environment that strengthens academic excellence while encouraging strong, supportive relationships between teachers and students. This school would focus on innovative educational practices as well as build a community where students and parents feel valued and understood.

To meet the educational needs of students, the ideal school would have to prioritize personalized learning, designing the lessons to each students strengthens, interests, and learning styles. Through technology and differentiated instruction, educators could customize the learning experience for students so they're learning because it is more relevant and enjoyable. This also prepares them for the complexities of the world.

Reggie:

My ideal school will incorporate lessons and instructions that are relevant to meeting the educational needs of the students

---

in this century. Help students to understand the real purpose of attending school and how education can and will help them achieve their career goals.

In order to strengthen teacher-student relationships, the ideal school would stress social emotional learning as one of the components of the curriculum. SEL programs teach students skills like empathy, self-awareness, and effective communication. These skills are especially important for strengthening interpersonal relationships.

Andrea:

I would create a school that engages the learner through relevance and provides opportunities for learners to apply life skills so that they are prepared for the real world. For example, incorporate math skills by developing budgets for trips, or using science to find ways to explore caves or figure out the heights of mountains.

I would use Maslow's Hierarchy of Needs as well as Howard Gardner's Theory of Multiple Intelligences; these theories will become the foundation of strengthening student relationships. It is important to be transparent, listen to students, and show love and respect. This will help to build relationships with students.

Designing an ideal school requires taking a holistic approach that prioritizes not only academic excellence but also strong teacher-student relationships. By focusing on students' strengths, interests, and learning styles, as well as creating a supportive and inclusive environment, educators can increase students' academic performance and personal development.

THE IMPACT OF CONTEMPORARY TIMES ON TEACHING

A Personal Reflection

The times we are living in now have brought unprecedented changes into almost every aspect of life, including education. Technology has changed the way educators teach. With the increase in digital tools and online platforms, educators have access to a wealth of resources and innovative teaching methods, making education more accessible and flexible.

Kristy:

Teaching is what you make it. It is important to be flexible and have the ability to adapt.

These times have presented challenges. The shift to online teaching during the pandemic truly made everyone aware of the digital divide, with some students not having access to technology or the internet. These issues made it difficult to make sure that all students could receive a quality education.

Not interacting face to face impacted the social aspect of learning, making it hard to develop meaningful relationships and even harder to engage students. Teachers had to adapt quickly to the technologies and pedagogies, often with very little training and support, causing an increase of stress and burnout.

Andrea:

Unfortunately, the pandemic occurred, and it played a significant role on how teaching changed. All classes were taught virtually. During that time, there was not a lot of learning, and for teachers, not being in front of the class made it hard to create excitement and to engage with the students. When we returned to school, we thought that it would go back to how it was before the pandemic, however it did not.

Reggie:

Working with youth today, has been extremely difficult. Educators are competing with students who feel that they are entitled; everything is given to them, so they do not think that they have to work for anything; and we are working with students that have not developed any critical thinking skills.

In conclusion, teaching students in the 21st century can be challenging, especially with a growing sense of entitlement among some students. This mindset can stem from the instant gratification that technology provides. Educators may need to emphasize the value of hard work, resilience, and the importance of achieving goals. Encouraging a growth mindset and fostering a sense of responsibility can help counteract entitlement and promote a more engaged and motivated classroom environment.

Our Remarkable Educators

Andrea:

When I attended school, elementary school consisted of first through seventh grade, and high school was from eighth to twelve grades. During my school years, I was highly active in sports, modern dance, and school plays. The highlight for me was when I had a chance to introduce Ms. Monica Kaufman at our seventh grade promotional. I was very involved in extracurricular activities, and I graduated with honors from high school. Looking back, I am disappointed in myself for getting into a fight and cheating on a geometry and physics test.

Third grade for me was the best year. It was because of my third-grade teacher. She showed love and respect for all of her students. She was always encouraging, telling us that all we needed to do was to try, and that she believed in us. When you did something wrong, she would correct you by giving you a warm hug around your shoulders and explain what you did wrong.

Reggie:

Thinking back to my days attending school, I really cannot remember anything good. I am disappointed in myself because I really did not take advantage of exploring my skills and talents. I did not have any guidance. I really did not understand the purpose of being in school. I thought you only had two choices, either go or not attend. It seemed that people who attended school could talk about a teacher who inspired them or helped them to tap into something they were interested in, but there was no teacher or counselor that cared about me. No one in school took an interest in helping me figure things out.

I did not have a plan after graduation. I remember being told, "This will no longer be your address at the end of the summer." I did some research and made the decision to move to Atlanta. I had a few individuals and co-workers that saw how I interacted with young people and the positive relationships I was able to build with them. They asked me, "Have you thought about being a school counselor?" This had me thinking about my short- and long-term goals. Maybe this is what I am supposed to do, working with young people, helping them through their journey—something I wish I had when I was in school.

Kristy:

During my school years, I was active in school activities and sports. I was raised with my mother; however, I knew my father. Neither one of them showed any interest in nor supporting the activities I was involved in. I remember my senior night; it was my very last basketball game. It was bittersweet since I was on varsity all four years in high school. I called my dad and told him how important that night was, and how I really wanted him to be there to escort me onto the court. His exact words were, "I'll be there with bells on baby." I was so excited. On that night, I kept looking all through the gym, but he was nowhere in sight. When it was time for my name to be called, my boyfriend, came out of nowhere, he took my hand and escorted me onto the floor. I was so hurt that my dad did not come. However, my heart skipped a beat knowing there was a man in my life that cared.

When I was a senior, I knew that I would be following my siblings and work in a factory after I graduate. It was not until I walked in my senior enrichment class that I met the teacher who would have a powerful impact on my life. I remember every day she would greet the class with a smile, and it seemed that her words came to life when she spoke. Every time she shared information, I would look it up. I wanted to be just as smart as her. She talked about Historically Black Colleges (HBCU), and I had never heard of them. She talked about her experience at an HBCU and told us that we would gain so much from attending an HBCU. I applied and was accepted. I will always be grateful for the impact she had on my life.

NURTURING SUCCESS

*How Parents Propel Children
to Academic Achievement*

No Place Like Home

Parents and the home environment play a very important role in shaping a child's attitude, behavior, and overall approach to school. John H. Wherry, President of the Parent Institute, reported, "Studies show that children from birth to high school spend 105,120, or 13.36 percent, of their waking hours in school, which means that 86.64 percent of children's time is spent out of school, mainly at home."[1] Research consistently shows that children who get positive support from their parents or guardians are more likely to do well academically and develop the skills to face the challenges of the world.

Home is the First School

Before children walk through the school doors, their educational journey begins at home. Parents are the first teachers; they are the ones to provide them with the foundational skills and attitudes that have an impact on their academic success.

---

1 John H. Wherry, *The influence of Home on School Success.*
https:::://www.naesp.org Sept/ Oct 2004, viewed July 5, 2024.

Parents have the responsibility to create a safe environment and experiences that encourage learning. The home environment shapes how children perceive and interact with the world around them.

The Power of Parental Involvement

When parents are actively involved in their child's education, it can increase their academic achievement, encourage positive behavior and improve their social skills. This involvement can include:

➤ Helping with homework.

➤ Spending time together.

➤ Attending parent-teacher conferences.

➤ Being actively involved in school activities or events.

➤ Positive reinforcement.

➤ Actively listening to your child.

When parents and guardians are involved, it sends the message that learning is very important.

Creating A Positive Learning Environment

It is important to create a supportive environment at home. Parents and guardians can:

> ➢ Provide a quiet space for studying.

> ➢ Demonstrate ways to balance school and self-time.

> ➢ Be a role model by showing a positive attitude towards learning.

> ➢ Demonstrate effective time management and organizational skills.

Building a Partnership with Schools

For children to succeed academically, parents and schools need to become partners. Both need to be in consistent communication so that they can identify and address any challenges early, making sure that the child receives the support needed.

The Foundation of Learning

Parents and guardians provide the foundation for how their children gravitate to education. From birth, parents and guardians can instill a love for learning by creating a stimulating and supportive environment, by including activities that promote cognitive development and encourage inquisitive conversations. Establishing a daily routine, limiting their time on social media, and teaching children about dedication and resilience.

Parents and guardians are a child's first and most influential teachers. The experiences and lessons they learn at home shape their cognitive, social, and emotional growth. This is why they need to create an environment that reinforces learning, and positive study habits and strengthens their love for learning.

It is important to keep the lines of communication open with your children. This helps to strengthen their emotional and psychological well-being. Communication enhances a trusting relationship and creates a space where children feel safe to express their thoughts, fears, concerns, and dreams. When children are allowed to be transparent without judgment, parents can better understand their experiences, be able to provide support, and address any issues they are having early. Honest conversations build a strong bond and can encourage mutual respect, helping children understand that they are valued and are being heard.

> **Mayra, mother of two:**
>
> I keep the lines of communication open. I encourage my sons to inform me of anything that they are having problems with, and together we find solutions. I encourage them to spend less time on social media, find hobbies, and spend more time as a family.
>
> Establishing a routine plays an important role in a child's academic success. Routines provide structure, which improves

a child's time management skills as well as a sense of responsibility. Having regular time to study, adequate rest, and balanced activities help children focus and retain information. It can reduce stress and anxiety.

Ju 'Reika, mother of one:

It is important to set up routines at an early age. I decided that it was important for me to set up routines for him. He has a routine for his meals, bedtime, and times we spend together doing some educational activities.

Christi, mother of two and grandmother of two:

When my son struggled in math, I reached out to the school for support, however when I did not get any help, I was able to find someone to tutor him. This helped him pass. When my daughter got pregnant, she was embarrassed and wanted to leave school. I did not want her to follow in my footsteps, so I kept her encouraged and motivated.

Supporting and encouraging your children involves a combination of active involvement, positive reinforcement, and keeping them motivated. Parents should spend quality time with their children and show interest in their activities and what is going on in school.

Celebrate their achievements no matter how small. It is important to strengthen their confidence while providing constructive feedback and helping them set realistic goals. Showing your support helps them to develop a powerful sense of self-worth and build up their resilience.

Encouraging curiosity in children is a powerful way to improve a child's critical thinking skill. This helps them explore ideas, become interested in learning more about the world, increase their ability to cope with complex problems, and adapt to change. Parents can stimulate their curiosity by creating an environment that is filled with books, educational activities/toys, and opportunities for hands-on learning. By valuing their children's innate curiosity, parents inspire a love for learning which will benefit them in all areas of life.

Managing School Challenges

Academic and Social Struggles

When managing the challenges a child faces at school, parents and guardians must take a proactive and empathetic approach. When your child is struggling in a subject, you must identify the reason why they are struggling. It will be important to communicate with their teachers to get their perspectives on where the support is needed. Teachers can provide strategies and resources that can help your child gain a better understanding on what subject they are having problems in. Also look at what is being offered in school, for example, tutoring or online resources that can provide additional support.

When addressing social issues like bullying or difficulty making friends, it is important to actively listen to your child's concerns and experiences. Parents and guardians must teach effective coping strategies, such as how to solve problems and being assertive. These skills can empower your child to deal with social challenges.

Parents and guardians have the responsibility for helping to navigate the challenges their children are experiencing during their school years. Challenges from academics to social dynamics can feel overwhelming for children and parents, but with the right approach, they can be manageable. Here are a few tips that can help you work through school-related challenges:

Communication

Establish open communication and encourage your children to talk about their day and any problems they might be having. Listen attentively to what your child has to say. Maintain a good relationship with their teacher.

Ju 'Reika:

I am working on my son's social skills. I am helping him with how to express himself without throwing a tantrum. I am finding that when I encourage him to tell me what is going on, he becomes calm. I had no one spend time helping me work on my social skills.

Mayra:

I am always encouraging my sons to do better than I did in school. I left school before I graduated. So, I am always sharing with them on hard it will be without a high school diploma. I continually check on their progress in school, and if they are having problems in a subject, I make sure that they attend tutorials when they are offered.

Understanding the Challenges

Identify any academic struggles your child is having. Work with the teachers and ask for additional resources or tutoring.

Be aware of any social problems. Encourage positive interaction. Take notice of any signs of anxiety, depression, or behavioral issues. Teach children coping skills. Seek professional help, if needed, and create a supportive home environment.

Christi:

I made sure that I was an involved parent. Every time the school would call, I would go up. I do that now with my grandchildren. I encouraged my children and grandchildren to share with me about their day in school and any challenges they were having.

Parents and guardians need to be proactive, empathic, and listening attentively. Stay engaged with their educational journey, work with the teachers and school counselors therefore you will be able to address issues effectively. Providing a supportive and understanding environment empowers children with the skills they need to overcome obstacles.

Overcoming Barriers

Strengthening Parent Engagement with Teachers and Staff

Parents and guardians are responsible for guiding their children through their educational journey. This requires collaboration between parents, teachers, and school staff. However, barriers can hinder parents and teachers from working together. It is important to understand and work through these barriers. By identifying the challenges and exploring together possible solutions, parents and teachers can create a more inclusive and effective partnership that prioritizes the success of every student.

Common Barriers

➤ Lack of communication between parents and teachers can lead to misunderstandings and missed opportunities to provide support to the student.

➤ Busy schedules for both the parent and teacher tend to make meetings difficult.

> Diverse backgrounds and languages can create obstacles.

> Previous negative experiences or perceptions can lead to a lack of trust.

Ju 'Reika:

My son is in daycare, and this is his first experience with school. I have already had some negative encounters with my son's teachers. I do understand that two-year-olds have a tough time expressing themselves and will get mad and have a tantrum. I have found myself always explaining to the teachers how to calm my son down, yet they keep yelling at him. I am not sure whether they are not listening to me because I am so young; however, they should respect me, regardless of my age. I can only imagine what is going to happen when he enters grade school.

Improving Communication

> Establish a way to communicate with teachers about your child's progress, events, and any problems they may be having. This can be done through emails or online school portals.

> Parents should share insights and concerns.

> Make sure that communication from both parties is clear and concise.

Mayra:

Sometimes dealing with teachers has been challenging. I have encountered teachers who chose not to talk with me. I have encountered teachers with bad attitudes. I do understand that teaching can be stressful. However, I keep trying to talk with teachers in order to support my children's academic journey.

Strengthening the Parent-School Partnership

Enhancing Student Success Together

The collaboration between parents and school staff creates the foundation of a supportive school community where students can thrive academically, socially, and emotionally. By promoting a strong partnership, parents, guardians, and school staff contribute significantly to the holistic development of every student. Keeping the lines of communication open, sharing goals, and striving to understand one another create a more cohesive system to maximize student achievement. Here are some suggestions:

Open and Regular Communication

➤ Stay informed; regularly check emails and school portals for updates.

➤ Keep open lines of communication with teachers and school staff. Share concerns and listen to their insight and feedback.

Mayra:

School staff needs to do a better job of communicating with parents, and not just when a student is in trouble. Keep parents informed of what is going on in the school of the school, do not wait until the last minute. As parents, we need to visit the schools more, and not just when there is an event like a concert or sports game. Teachers need to keep in mind that communicating with parents is for the success of all students.

Ju 'Reika:

Parents and school staff need to communicate and listen to one another. Work together to help the students stay excited about school.

Christi:

Parents and school staff need to work together and communicate more than just when a student gets in trouble. Maybe offer sessions for parents, providing strategies on how to work with their children at home.

Get Involved

➢ Stay engaged by participating in parent-teacher conferences.

➢ Volunteer when you have the time. This helps you to stay connected with the school community, and it shows that you are committed to making a positive impact.

➢ Support school initiatives that promote cultural awareness.

Show Appreciation and Respect

➢ Acknowledge the efforts of teachers and school staff. Positive feedback goes a long way.

➢ Respect teachers' professional boundaries. Find a meeting time that works for both parent and teacher.

Problem-Solve Together

➢ When issues come up, address them immediately, and come to the meeting with a problem-solving mindset.

➢ Collaborate with the school staff to develop strategies to address any academic or social issues early.

Stay Informed

➤ Familiarize yourself with school policies and expectations. This will help you advocate for your child.

➤ Promote a positive attitude towards education.

➤ Voice concerns and suggestions respectfully to the school staff to help shape a positive learning environment.

Strengthening parent-school relationships is vital for the educational success of children. When both work together, a cohesive support system that addresses the academic and emotional needs of students is formed. Involved parents can provide insights into their children's strengths and challenges, helping teachers design strategies to meet the educational needs of students. Additionally, positive collaboration between parents and school staff promotes a positive school community where students feel motivated to do their best.

Meet The Parents

Mayra:

My sisters and I were raised in a two-parent household. My parents are immigrants. The home environment was not the best, filled with arguments and violence. My dad suffered from alcoholism, and my mother had to provide everything for the home and the family.

School was not easy for us. We never had the resources or anyone to help us with homework or projects. There was no one to check with teachers on how we were doing, and teachers never reached out to our parents. I was always falling behind in school. It was so frustrating.

I became pregnant at an early age, and when my first child was born, I dropped out of school. I am the proud parent of two sons, one in high school and one in middle school. My oldest feels indifference to school. He would rather work than go to school. He does not understand how school is going to help him. My youngest feels anxious about school, especially with the increase in school threats. Social media does not help. Neither feel safe in school.

Ju 'Reika:

It has not been that long since I left high school. I had some good moments and bad moments in school. I enjoyed making friends and participating in sports. I remember getting bullied a lot, which kept me involved in drama. I found myself arguing and losing my temper. It seemed that teachers and school staff did not care about what I was going through. All they were interested in was who they were going to suspend. I decided to quit school.

I am a seventeen-year-old with a two-year-old son. He is my pride and joy. I take being a parent seriously. I work and have enrolled in a program to help me obtain my high school equivalency diploma. I need to get my diploma so I can encourage my son to finish high school.

Although my son is only two, I need to set the tone of how important education is. Currently, he enjoys going to daycare. It is my job to help him stay excited about school and his education. I only wish that someone cared enough about me to help me understand why education was so important.

Christi:

I grew up in a single-parent household with an overprotective mother. I knew my mother loved me, yet she needed to know every move I made. If I wanted to go over to a friend's house, she had to know everything about their parents. Whenever

I would say or get an answer wrong, my mom would pop me. When I look back, that is probably why I am always second-guessing myself.

School was not a pleasant experience for me. I was bullied in middle school. I was held back, and I started to believe that I was not smart enough. I did not have anyone in the school who encouraged me or helped me. When I went to high school, I began skipping class. My mom moved me from school to school, but it did not matter, I was still doing what I wanted to do. Finally, my mom gave up. When I got pregnant, I dropped out of school.

Now, as a mother of two, I am determined that even though I did not finish school, I want to make sure that both of my children finish high school. To set the expectation, I returned to school to complete my education.

EMPOWERING STUDENT VOICES

Students' Impact on Education

Student voices are important in creating an engaging, inclusive, and effective school community. Encouraging students to express their opinions, ideas, and concerns, confirming their experiences, increases their motivation and commitment to learn. Empowering students gives them a sense of ownership over their education. When students feel heard and respected, their critical thinking, communication, and advocacy skills improve.

Schools that incorporate students' voices in the decision-making process help to develop a more democratic and equitable school culture, helping to address inequities and ensure that the needs of all students, especially those from marginalized groups, are considered. Empowering students to have a voice in shaping their educational experiences helps to develop their leadership skills and prepares them to become active and productive citizens.

Parents and school staff can enhance student voices by integrating them into the decision-making processes, actively seeking feedback from them, and creating platforms for students to participate.

For parents, start by actively listening to your children. Encourage them to share their experiences in school and advocate for their needs. Allowing your children to communicate with you helps them feel confident to advocate for themselves in school. Parents can partner with the teachers and administrators to provide feedback and insight regarding their children's perspectives, thus contributing to a responsive, student-centered school community.

Teachers, counselors, and administrators can work with the parents to create a school community that prioritizes student input. Teachers can incorporate student choices and voices into their lesson plans and classroom management strategies, helping to ensure that students have input regarding their learning. By working together, parents and school staff can create a collaborative approach that empowers students to feel valued and heard.

Schools can create a more engaging, equitable, and effective school climate by providing opportunities for students to share their ideas and concerns.

Students' Insights and Perspectives

In this section, we explore reflections of students on various aspects of their school experiences. Each student, regardless of background or circumstances, were asked a series of thought-provoking questions and asked to share their overall experiences in school.

Essence:

I had the opportunity to visit many different regions and cities, and when people ask me where I am from, I respond, "Everywhere." My sisters and I were raised by our mother; however, I had an amazing father present in my life. I do not think I valued the impact he had on me until he passed in 2022. I feel his presence every day.

My support system consists of my grandparents, aunts, uncles, and cousins. Although we do not speak every day, we have such an enjoyable time when we get together. I am always finding the bright side of any situation. Growing up, I did not like it when people were cruel to others, and the best part of growing up was being able to be with people who cared about me, and we would just laugh.

Throughout my school years, I participated in quite a few programs that helped me to build my leadership skills. For example, I participated in community events, spoke at Black history programs, and competed in a variety of activities. All the opportunities that I engaged in were because of my mother's love and encouragement.

I remember a time when I shared with the principal about an issue I was concerned about, and when I asked for a solution in reference to the issue, the principal was dismissive, and I was told to talk with a teacher. When I went to the teacher's classroom, before I opened my mouth I was told, "Nobody is allowed to enter the room, and everyone knows that!" Although the issue was not resolved that never stopped me from trying to make positive changes; however, it did change my view of the administrative team and how they dismissed students' voices. This was my first lesson about adults' perspectives with young people. It showed me that people only care about what is important to themselves and to make a change you must be in a position to make that decision. I must admit, my positive and negative experiences during my school years have shaped me into the best individual I could be.

Q. If you could share your thoughts about school with teachers and administrators, what would that be?

A. I would want them to know that each student's perspective of learning is important and different. Acknowledge, respect, and conduct classes that reflect that.

Q. Given a chance, what is one change that you would like to see in school?

A. I would like to see the structure of the school change. Current school policies contribute to the lack of student success. The policies need to be updated to better address the needs of the current generation.

Q. What did you find challenging about your experience in school?

A. My experiences with different energies and out-of-school related issues that are played out in school, and how those issues dictated how the school day would go.

Q. What happens in school that makes you afraid and frustrated? When that happens, what can adults do to provide support?

A. I would get frustrated with the easy access to the school building. This does not make students feel safe. The school needs to stop wasting money on updating metal detectors and find better ways to secure the school. Adults need to include students in ways to secure the building. They would be surprised by what students know. After all, students are the ones sneaking in and out.

Q. What makes you feel the most appreciated and understood?

A. What makes me feel appreciated the most is expressing my thoughts and feelings and receiving either understanding or acknowledgment.

Q. What adult can you talk to when needed? What qualities do they have that make it easy to talk with?

A. The person I go to when I need to talk is my mother. My mom knows me the best and always has my best interest at heart.

Alexis:

I am the oldest of four siblings. I have two younger sisters and a younger brother. We are Hispanic. My parents do not speak English, yet they are making great strides in learning the language. We are a remarkably close family, and I cherish my relationship with them.

All the good memories of my childhood involve my immediate family. I remember that we went to the beach for my brother's birthday. Nothing happened out of the ordinary, just being with the family, I had the best time. I had been thinking about learning to play the guitar, and it meant a lot to me when I finally purchased one. I remember when one Christmas my brother and I spent time on the skateboard. We decided to go down a big hill, and I fell and broke my wrist. I spent two months in a cast.

I enjoyed elementary school. I liked my teachers and my classmates. I did experience teasing from a boy for a couple of months; however, that taught me to be more assertive with how I was feeling and be vocal about any problems I was experiencing. In middle school, I made a few more friends, joined clubs, and expanded my interests. I remember the time in middle school when I decided to join the debate team. Being on the debate team, my self-confidence improved, and I learned to be more vocal. High school was different. When I started high school, we had classes virtually due to the pandemic. One good thing about having classes online was I was able to focus on my hobbies and interests, particularly the guitar. One of the hardest experiences was that with virtual learning, we spent a year in isolation. When we finally went back to classes in the building, I had to learn to multitask, be more responsible, and to make friends.

Q. If you could share your thoughts about school with teachers and administrators, what would it be?

A. I felt the issues in the school, for the most part, were because of the students. The problems I encountered in school were caused by the students. Teachers and administrators should work on finding out the root of the problem and work with students to create positive solutions. Something I did not like about school was the lack of communication that often occurred between different teachers. I wish teachers would work together and assign work in manageable chucks. Teachers will often assign multiple assignments and only grade a select few. This burdens students with unnecessary work that is never graded.

Q. Given a chance, what is one change that you would like to see in school?

A. The one change I would like to see schools create is a study block. This would allow the students an opportunity to either finish homework or complete a project. Schools do not need to make students take unnecessary classes just to fill up a space.

Q. What did you find challenging about your experience in school?

A. For me, it was time management. I tend to be a procrastinator, which kept me stressed all of the time because I was always trying to do the work at the last minute.

Q. What happens in school that makes you afraid and frustrated? When that happens, what adults can do to provide support?

A. Nothing in school really makes me afraid, but I often find myself frustrated with the repetitive nature in school. Also,

I get frustrated with morning classes because I find it hard to concentrate.

Q. What makes you feel the most appreciated and understood?

A. I feel most appreciated when someone I am speaking to shows genuine interest in what I am saying. I can tell if someone is interested in what I am saying or if someone is just being polite.

Q. What adult can you talk to when needed? What qualities do you think they have that make it easy to talk with?

A. When I need to talk with someone, I turn to my parents. My parents are people I can trust, and I know they will sincerely try to help me out. It is important to trust whoever you confide in.

Jayla:

My family consists of my dad, grandfather, my grandmother, and my great grandmother. I spent most of my school years with my grandmother because my dad works and lives out of state, yet he stays involved in all aspects of my life. My family kept me involved in extracurricular activities. This helped me stay focused in my personal life and my academics. The members of my family stress the importance of education. They encourage me to get the best grades and not settle for less. I love my family because when I make mistakes and seem to get off track, they are always there to make sure I get back on the right track.

I have so many good childhood memories, especially the times I spent with my dad, grandfather, grandmother, and great grandmother. Because of my family, I had the chance to travel to a variety of places and have had some amazing experiences. In elementary and middle school, I was getting good grades and cheering. Looking back, I do regret some decisions that I made; however, I did learn from them.

High school was a challenge. The schoolwork was harder, and there were quite a few distractions. I learned that the best way to get through high school is to just do your work, focus on getting to college, and then your life will begin.

I had amazing support from teachers. All my teachers loved me, and I could talk with them about everything. I thought I was close to the administrators, until I got into my first fight at school, it seemed that the school system failed me because they didn't seem to care. It did not matter that it was my first time getting in trouble. I did not feel any support. This all happened because I was supporting my friend in a situation which resulted in a fight breaking out. At that time, I did not realize that decision would mess up my life. Now that I look back, I should have done what I had been doing all along, that was minding my own business. I have learned a lot in my life and with the love and support from my family, I will stay on the right track to succeed. Mistakes provide life lessons.

Q. If you could share your thoughts about school with teachers and administrators, what would that be?

A. By providing support, teachers and administrators can help students succeed. However, in order for that to happen, they need to understand the challenges that students face, as well as take into consideration the mental health of students.

Q. Given a chance, what is the one change that you would like to see in school?

A. I would like to see more people that specialized in talking with Black youth and helping them work through tough situations. Not everyone understands Black youth and what they have been through.

Q. What did you find challenging about your experience in school?

A. For me, it was hard staying on top of my work and not getting distracted.

Q. What happens in school that makes you afraid and frustrated? When that happens, what can the adults do to better provide support?

A. I feel afraid when schools do not take school threats seriously. I become frustrated when schools do not cancel due to the weather even though other schools have cancelled, and not having people that can help you through traumatic experiences. Adults can better support students by actually listening.

Q. What makes you feel the most appreciated and understood?

A. When I get the chance to explain my side of the story and I am actually heard.

Q. What adult can you talk to when needed? What qualities do they have that make it easy to talk to?

A. My father and grandfather. Because of their life experiences, they actually understand, and they do not yell when I talk with them about things and the mistakes I have made.

Jaylan:

I was raised in a two-parent household. My family means the world to me. Growing up, I felt extremely comfortable with my family. I am remarkably close to my siblings, even though my sister and I are ten years apart. Together, my family and I created memories that I cherish to this day. One of my favorite memories is when my mother and father noticed that I had an interest in art, maybe because I was always drawing and coloring. My father became my mentor, teaching me different techniques. My mother was the one that I could share my ideas with, and she provided me with career ideas for when I graduated from high school. My family and I have an extraordinarily strong bond. I feel loved and supported. With my family, I knew that I could overcome any challenges that I faced.

When I think back to school, I have had some good experiences and some not so good. In elementary school, I had some teachers who took a bullying approach when working with the students. I remember having trouble with another student and when I talked to the teacher, nothing was done, the teacher allowed the student to keep teasing me. When I had enough, I snapped, and I was the one who got in trouble. Going to middle school was a completely different world. Seventh grade was probably the worst year for me. I became depressed and even had suicidal thoughts. To this day, I am thankful for my parents, and my art teacher. He was the only teacher who noticed that I was struggling and kept assuring me that it would get better. He promised me that he would not let me fall into a pit of darkness. He gave me new art supplies and occasionally reached out to my parents to let them know how I was doing.

School became better until the pandemic took over my first year in high school. We attended classes virtually; however, once we were back in the building everything slowly become normal. All that came after I started making friends, learning how to balance class and homework, and thinking about my next move after high school. Although it was extremely stressful, I did enjoy my years in high school, and I am striving towards greatness.

Q. If you could share your thoughts about school with teachers and administrators, what would that be?

A. Teachers and administrators, we do appreciate the ones who care about the students; however, some teachers spend more time getting a little too close, trying to be a friend. Those teachers need to find a balance.

Q. Given a chance, what is one change that you would like to see in school?

A. I would like to see more opportunities for students to be able to express themselves, as I believe it gives students a sense of being responsible for their education and strengthens the school community.

Q. What did you find challenging about your experience in school?

A. I found making friends difficult because so many people are self-centered or are too afraid to open up.

Q. What happens in school that makes you afraid and frustrated? When that happens, what can adults do to provide support?

A. I got frustrated with cyberbullying in school. Social media has made it easy for cyberbullying to happen. Students can harass other students and stay anonymous, sometimes encouraging students to end their own lives. Adults could do more by tracking down who is involved and consistently reminding students about the dangers of social media and the consequences.

Q. What makes you feel the most appreciated and understood?

A. I feel the most appreciated and understood when I talk with people who I have a good relationship with people who care about me, who want the best for me, and will be truthful with me.

Q. What adult can you talk to when needed? What qualities do they have that make it easy to talk with?

A. When I need to talk, I would go to my mom or dad. My parents are always willing to help me, always providing a safe space for me to express myself, and for that, I am eternally grateful.

*
**

Through these student perspectives, it is clear that students are keen observers of their school community who can be valuable contributors to improving the environment. Teachers and administrators should be open to listening to student voices and try implementing some changes that they suggest, for they may find that it creates a more inclusive and supportive school.

Student feedback can transform the educational experience by providing educators with information on how effective the course content and overall classroom environment are. By seeking out feedback from students, teachers can identify areas that need improvement, search out new strategies to better meet students' needs, and create a more engaging learning atmosphere.

This collaborative approach empowers students by giving them a sense of ownership in their education.

BLUEPRINT FOR TEACHERS

AND PARENTS

Strategies for Collaboration

Effective collaboration between parents and teachers is extremely important for a student's academic success. Here are several strategies that can help to strengthen this collaboration:

Teachers

➢ Get to know parents individually and understand their perspectives, concerns, and what are their expectations.

➢ Share positive news and accomplishments regularly.

➢ Highlight students' strengths and improvements, not just the challenges they are facing.

➢ Provide regular updates about students' progress through emails or a class website. Consider using digital tools like messaging apps and school portals for efficient communication.

➤ Schedule meetings to talk about students' progress and address any concerns. Offer flexible times to accommodate different schedules.

➤ Provide guidelines for parents on how to help with assignments. Provide resources and tools to support learning at home.

➤ Share information about upcoming workshops that are offered on various educational topics such as technology use.

➤ Make sure parents feel comfortable reaching out to teachers with questions or concerns.

➤ Be approachable and available for informal discussions.

Parents

➤ When your schedule permits, visit schools, participate in activities, volunteer for events, and share your skills and hobbies.

➤ Encourage your students to express their academic and emotional needs.

➤ Check emails, school portals, and apps to stay informed about your students' assignments, grades, and upcoming events.

➢ Listen to teachers' insights and concerns without being defensive. This will create a more productive dialogue.

➢ Know the teachers' policies on homework, attendance, behavior, dress codes, and cell phones.

➢ Show that you value education through your words and actions.

➢ Work with the teacher to develop strategies to address concerns. If you notice any issues, address them immediately.

➢ Be an active member of the PTA so you will have a voice in school policies and activities.

➢ Encourage your child to do their best and emphasize that it is important to take pride in their work.

➢ Recognize that teachers are trained professionals and can provide insights into the students' education.

➢ Strengthen the student's communication, cooperation, and conflict resolution skills.

➢ If your child needs extra help, seek out the supportive services at the school.

➢ Be attentive to your child's emotional needs. Work with the school to provide additional support if it is needed.

> Create a positive learning environment at home.

> Show appreciation to teachers and school staff for their support.

Build a Supportive Environment

> Parents and teachers should work with the student to set realistic academic goals. Regularly reviewing the goals will help the student to stay on track.

> Parents and teachers should practice active listening and respect each other's perspectives.

> For students who need extra help, develop an individualized learning plan with input from both teachers and parents to ensure that the students' academic needs are being met.

> When issues come up, teachers and parents should work together to develop solutions for the best interests of the child.

> Make sure that both home and school environments are consistent regarding expectations and even disciplinary actions. It is important for students to understand the expectations and boundaries.

➤ Use technology for virtual meetings when parents cannot attend in person meetings.

➤ Both parents and teachers should recognize students' achievement, no matter how small. Positive reinforcement motivates students to keep trying.

TAKING CHARGE

TIPS FOR STUDENTS TO ACHIEVE ACADEMIC SUCCESS

Achieving academic success involves developing effective study habits, time management skills, and ways to take care of oneself. Here are some strategies that will help your students succeed:

Habits to Develop

> ➤ Students need to engage in active learning. This includes summarizing, questioning, and discussing.

> ➤ Incorporate the technique SQ3R: Survey, Question, Read, Recite, Review for reading and comprehension.[2]

> ➤ Set regular study times.

> ➤ Find and use a note-taking system.

---

2 Francis P. Roberson, "Effective Study" January 1, 1961, https://www.mind-tools.com, viewed July 17,2024.

> Review materials to reinforce learning.

> Seek help from teachers if you are having difficulties in a subject.

Time Management

> Focus on high priority tasks first.

> Use a digital calendar to keep up with assignments and deadlines.

> Avoid procrastination by breaking tasks into manageable steps so that you will not feel overwhelmed.

> Use a timer to break up study time into intervals followed by a break. This will help you to maintain being productive.

Self-Care

> Be sure to get enough sleep, eat healthy, and exercise.

> Learn how to manage stress through relaxation techniques like deep breathing, developing a hobby, and limiting the time you spend on social media. If you need additional help, talk with your parents or an adult at school that you trust.

Home Environment

➤ Choose a quiet area to use as a study space.

➤ Make sure you have everything you need.

➤ Turn off your electronic devices during the times you are studying and engaging with the teachers.

➤ Keep parents informed with your progress, achievements, and challenges.

➤ Share your goals with your parents to keep them informed.

➤ Know that your parents will be your emotional support and encouragement, especially during stressful times.

Attitude

➤ Develop a growth mindset by embracing challenges and looking at mistakes as opportunities to learn.

➤ Stay resilient, especially when facing challenges.

➤ Set short-term and long-term goals. This helps you to stay on track.

Academic Skills

➤ Strengthen your critical thinking and problem-solving skills.

➤ Question assumptions and evaluate evidence critically.

➤ Work on your writing skills.

➤ Keep teachers informed about any challenges you may be facing.

➤ Request feedback on assignments and projects. This will help you strengthen your skills.

➤ Engage in class discussions.

Resources

➤ Take advantage of any resources provided by your teacher.

➤ If you need help, attend review sessions and/or tutorials.

➤ Use online platforms, for example, Khan Academy.

➤ Use libraries; they offer study spaces, online databases, and resources.

➤ Form study groups.

Authors

Debra Tavaras, CEO of Soulstice Inc. has over thirty years of experience with education and nonprofits. Debra received her bachelor's degree from Georgia State University, MBA from American InterContinental University, and ED.S from Walden University. Soulstice Inc. programs have received recognition from the 44th President and Vice President of the United States and a letter of congratulations from the 60th Mayor of Atlanta. She is the co-author of the 2019 book *Building Bridges: 10 Steps to Engage Youth*, and author of the 2022 journal "What A Year!" and the article "In the Halls of Justice: The Educational Value of Moot Court" published in TEACHMEDIA.

Bevin Carpenter, CEO of Building Bridges Consulting LLC, also known as the "Guru of Engagement," has over twenty-five years' experience working with K–12 and post-secondary education. He received his bachelor's degree from the University of Memphis and his MBA from Strayer University. He has served on several boards and facilitated workshops and programs for students, parents, communities, and agencies. His article "Empowering Students to be Change Agents" was published by *Youth Today*. He is the author of the 2019 book *Building Bridges: 10 Steps to Engage Youth*, and co-author of the 2022 journal "What A Year!"

For additional information, Mr. Carpenter can be reached at: www.bb2connect.com.

Contributors

Educators
Andrea Carter
Reggie Carter
Kristy A. Taylor

Parents
Ju 'Reika Ross
Christi Sanders
Mayra Vazquez

Students
Jayla Carpenter
Jaylan Smith
Essence Stephens
Alexis Hernandez-Tellez